ENDORSEMENTS

The Proof is in the Pudding!
STATS 2013-2014

Timeframe	3rd Grade (STAAR Scores)	4th Grade (STAAR Scores)	5th Grade (STAAR Scores)
Prior Year Data	21%	17%	37%
During my regime	58%	71%	67%

STATS 2014-2015

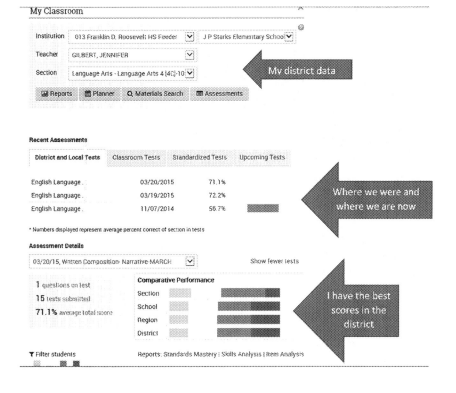

STATS 2014-2015 part 2

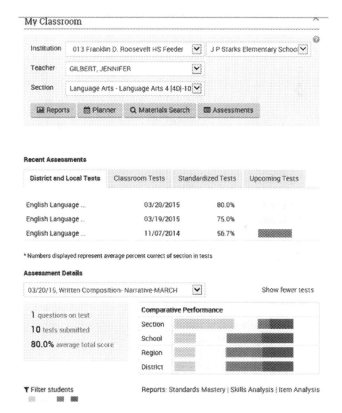

STATS 2015-2016

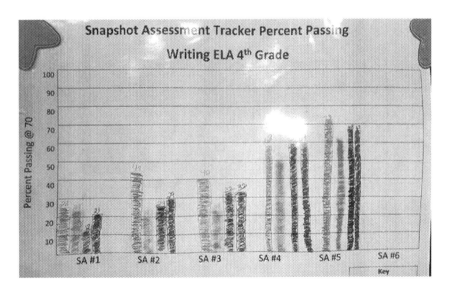

THE
DATA-DRIVEN
INSTRUCTIONAL CLASSROOM
TEACHING WITH PURPOSE AND PASSION

DR. JENNIFER GILBERT

iUniverse®

THE DATA-DRIVEN INSTRUCTIONAL CLASSROOM
TEACHING WITH PURPOSE AND PASSION

iUniverse books may be ordered through booksellers or by contacting:

iUniverse
1663 Liberty Drive
Bloomington, IN 47403
www.iuniverse.com
1-800-Authors (1-800-288-4677)

Because of the dynamic nature of the Internet, any web addresses or links contained in this book may have changed since publication and may no longer be valid. The views expressed in this work are solely those of the author and do not necessarily reflect the views of the publisher, and the publisher hereby disclaims any responsibility for them.

Any people depicted in stock imagery provided by Thinkstock are models, and such images are being used for illustrative purposes only. Certain stock imagery © Thinkstock.

ISBN: 978-1-5320-2464-1 (sc)
ISBN: 978-1-5320-2463-4 (e)

Library of Congress Control Number: 2017909491

Print information available on the last page.

iUniverse rev. date: 06/28/2017

Card Series and Title Page
<u>Also by Jennifer Gilbert</u>

Churchin' Ain't Easy (2011)

...And Deliver Us From People! (2013)

For the Perfecting of the Saints (2014)

365 Revelatory Words for Any Given Day (2017)

Help! My Students Are Bored And So Am I! (2017)

The Journey Back to Me (2017)

Teach Me How to Live Realistically Single (2017)

DEDICATION

This book is dedicated to all of the teachers who want to see results. Those teachers who want to see the fruits of their labor immediately. To the strategists that understand the politics, but more appreciate the process and the lifelong impact that learning brings about. To the teacher that is determined to see results and want to make a difference. As a fellow educator that is still in the classroom, I know the struggle of how to effectively pull it all together, this book is for you. I hope it helps make the load a little lighter.

EPIGRAPH

Teachers teach from the heart and a place of pure passion, and not just from the book for the sake of a test!

-Dr. Jennifer Gilbert

CONTENTS

FOREWORD

As the Reading Language Arts Campus Instructional Coach at J.P. Starks Math, Science & Technology Vanguard, I am writing in recommendation for Dr. Jennifer Gilbert.

I have known Dr. Gilbert since the 2014-2015 academic school year as a 4th grade RLA Vanguard teacher at J.P. Starks Math, Science & Technology Vanguard. Her drive and spirited personality sets her apart from other teachers. She has a gladiator mentality and has high expectations for her students. Her high energy classroom says a lot about the culture of her classroom environment. There is not a day that goes by where Dr. Gilbert's students are not engaged, energized, having fun with learning, but also being challenged.

Portraying a great asset for being a teacher of a vanguard program within a regular-ed school comes with great accomplishments and consistent quality instruction that challenges her students. She has proven the ability of promoting a positive, caring climate for learning that nurtures all children's cultural backgrounds and various academic strengths and weakness. Her instructional abilities have profound measurable student gains and closure of student achievement gaps in critical thinking reading skills, specifically with ESL students. Lessons are data-driven with student-created learning profiles and data trackers. Setting high standards for her students using enriched and accelerated rigorous instruction, challenges the students, which promotes their natural capacities for critical analysis and creative problem-solving. Dr. Gilbert's instruction consists of more than just textbooks, but the integration of technology, use of student created power-point presentations as tools for assessing comprehension of various content assignments, media literacy, and other innovative techniques for cross-content learning.

In addition to her excellent classroom instructional approaches, Dr. Gilbert goes the extra mile to ensure her students are beyond prepared for academic readiness. She sacrifices time to tutor students that need to be challenged as well as low performing student twice a week, takes part in Saturday school intervention, and provides incentives for not just academic achievement, but academic growth.

I assure you, Dr. Jennifer Gilbert is an educational gem that will make an impact on any child she encounters. She will be a great asset to any campus that seeks teachers of passion and commitment.

Best regards
Joy Runnels, M.Ed.

PREFACE

I remember when I first started teaching like it was yesterday. I had graduated college, passed all of my exams and I was now certified and ready to roll. I was ready to take on the world and change lives one student at a time. I was top of my class, so I just knew that I had it all figured out. WRONG!!! The truth of the matter is that I knew nothing.

Education has a way of changing as regularly as technology. Just like with technology, there is a new game system or operating system that comes out every year, so it is with the world of education. There is always a new law, methodology, political stance and the like. Every year that I teach I learn something new. I designed this book to assist in putting together the pieces of the puzzle that never changes: data and expectations.

Whether you are a common core state or not this book will assist in how to create an atmosphere that is stress free and works for you and your administrator, but most of all your students and their parents. This book will walk you from start to finish how to mesh all expectations together from the politics to the classroom application.

ACKNOWLEDGEMENTS

I acknowledge all of the administrators whom I have worked with along the way. Some of whom I agreed with and others not so much. Two administrators that I would like to honor by name are my first principal Dr. Berkiesha Needum Scott who pushed me to become one of the great teachers on her team. She walked me through my first year as a teacher of record and kept pushing me until I became one of the best on the market. The second principal that I want to honor is Dr. Tiffany Rock who encouraged me to stick with education when I thought that I couldn't and wouldn't go another day dealing with difficult parents and hard to please administration. She knew that her assignment from God for me was to work on my people skills and how to not take it personal when I wanted more for other people's children then their own parents did. I honor these ladies because no matter where I go in life I will always look up to them and aspire to be a version of their characteristics.

INTRODUCTION

How does this go with that? How do I track this while teaching that? Can I find all of my expectations in one place with all of the puzzle pieces put together that I can read, follow, and make sense of. Well now you can! Welcome to the world of educational K.I.S.S. (Keeping It Simple and Sensible). This book walks you through state expectations, school expectations, parent's expectations, student's expectations and self-expectations. Sounds like madness huh? Well here is the method to the madness in just a few words, "Numbers Don't Lie."

I have been teaching for a number of years in some of the largest districts in the state of Texas, and I have found one thing to be consistent, the expectations. It is my desire that this book will become a lifelong resource for years to come for new and old teachers that want to be strategic in their pursuits of educational success. We all want to see our students learn and we also want to see the fruits of our labor. We want to know, prior to an observation, whether or not our teaching was effective. This book is going to show you how to measure all of those things with ease and comfort. Scaffolding in all of the expectations that are placed on you, I would that this book be a one stop shop for all to see and use effectively and witness a direct benefit from. I don't want this to be another book that you sit on the shelf like the papers that we get from professional development and just let it collect dust and be a distant memory. However, I would that it help you to create a framework for your day to day teaching and how to make your year more successful and data driven.

TEACHER EXPECTATIONS GALORE

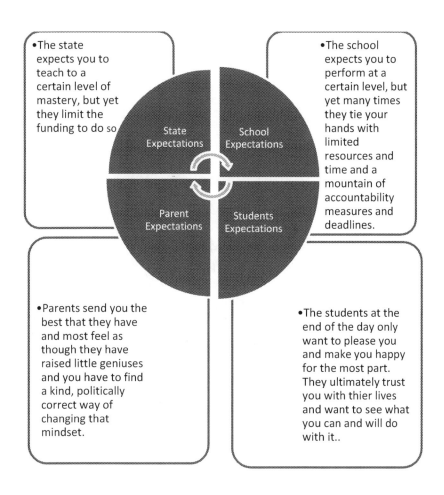

- The state expects you to teach to a certain level of mastery, but yet they limit the funding to do so.

State Expectations

- The school expects you to perform at a certain level, but yet many times they tie your hands with limited resources and time and a mountain of accountability measures and deadlines.

School Expectations

Parent Expectations

Students Expectations

- Parents send you the best that they have and most feel as though they have raised little geniuses and you have to find a kind, politically correct way of changing that mindset.

- The students at the end of the day only want to please you and make you happy for the most part. They ultimately trust you with thier lives and want to see what you can and will do with it..

Let's see how to make it all work!

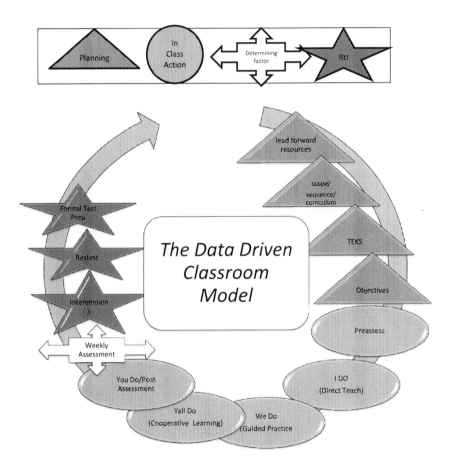

CHAPTER ONE

STATE EXPECTATIONS

Purpose*: *The state expectations are to outline what the student should know by the end of the given school year for that grade level.

When we speak of state expectations we are talking about what "they" (the state) says that a student should know with a certain level of mastery before the end of the given school year. These expectations are vertically aligned from grade to grade and grow in complexity as time goes on. For the sake of accountability, I always review state expectations for the current year, the prior year and the upcoming year to gauge what the student should already know, what I am responsible for teaching, and just how far to go into a single concept. I recommend reviewing the prior year so that you can know what to review before teaching the current year's concept. It will also help you to know what background knowledge needs to be imparted and if the students are doing well it won't hurt to tell them what they will learn later or you can always move your top students forward a bit and prepare the others to make a connection for the next year.

Looking ahead also allows you the opportunity to differentiate your instruction according to mastery. Lower levels will focus on prior year, mainstream will focus on current year expectations and the accelerated learner can start on next year's expectation. This is more of a natural progression of learning of the same concept just by adding a little rigor to the instructional plan.

These state expectations are used to create the standardized test that we will talk about later in the book. When the students are tested they are presumed to be on grade level and performing at mastery. State expectations are needed and if you don't think so imagine what the education system would look like if there were none. I know as a seasoned educator myself, there are those teachers that are not there for the education and the betterment of the students, but rather just enjoy the so called, "frequent breaks" that they think that we get with pay. The truth of the matter is that yes we get breaks and they are well deserved and always needed, but if the truth be told during summer, we are in training to catch up on the latest and greatest methodology to hit the market or some district changes that are being made. Most of the time during the breaks, we are spending time catching up on things that we fell behind on, be it business or personal affairs.

In 2009, a state-led effort created the common core craze that places expectations on a national level. Not all states have bought into it and many don't see the need for it, but I can honestly speak from experience when I say that I wish that they had started this years ago.

As a military child I was born in Oklahoma, raised in Europe, came back to the U.S. and lived in Georgia and I found myself, in addition to being the Talented and Gifted (TAG) student that I was, always a world ahead of the other students. Common core would help with issues such as that.

States such as Texas have not adopted the common core curriculum yet, and from the looks of it, Texas never will. While doing the research for this book I see why. Texas is ahead of the common core curriculum which will in turn keep our students "ahead" while the truth of the matter is that with the acceleration of the TEKS that they implemented a few years ago, many students are actually struggling and experiencing learning gaps that are yet to be filled. We are just now seeing the full effects of the increase of rigor that took place about two years ago. The learning gaps are being made manifest.

Common Core Debate	
For...	**Against...**
It makes sharing of resources a lot easier because all expectations would be the same.	Even though the expectations are the same the rigor and strategies can and will be different.
With the mobile society that we are becoming, keeping the expectation the same closes in some of the gaps that students experience in the move from one location to the other.	Even though the expectation is the same, the scope and sequence may be different which means that mobile students may come in with deficiencies even still.
This makes collaboration a lot easier on a national level between educators.	Yes collaboration is possible but standards may still differ within the framework of common core.
	There has been no formal training on the common core and the expectations that were taken into effect when they were implemented.

CHAPTER TWO

STANDARDIZED TESTING

Purpose: standardized testing can and should be used for many reasons for which we will cover in this chapter. Hopefully after being empowered with the correct way to use the information, you will be for standardized testing as well.

Now that you know what your state expectations are overall, now it is time to do our first breakdown. I am going to use Texas standards because that is where I teach. Some states are common core and others are not and Texas just happens to be a state that has not adopted the common core as of yet.

Many people have mixed emotions about the whole standardized testing piece as do I. I have mixed emotions because there is so much stress placed on the test that learning has lost its enjoyment. I have taught many grades that are testing grades and I see what the stress does to the children, the teachers, the parents and of course the administration.

I think standardized testing is a great way to measure where students are currently performing and I also believe that it should follow the students, but it should not be the entire picture of the students.

The three reasons standardized testing should be used are for;

- Prior year data
- Goal setting
- Data Tracking

Prior year data

Prior year's data can serve many purposes of which we will talk about.

Purpose: Prior year data should be used as a gauging tool to give the teacher some sort of idea of the student's ability. Some things have to be taken into consideration when looking at prior year data. Here are a list of dos and don'ts when using this information.

Dos And Don'ts For Using Prior Years Data	
Dos	Don'ts
Look for behavioral issues that should be of concern, not classroom management negligence, but real issues that could impede on the safety of the other students	Prejudge a students based on prior year's miniscule behavior
Look at prior scores and assessments to see what subject the students are weak and strong in and what some of the issues appear to be	Pregroup or prejudge students based on their prior scores
Have a discussion with students about their prior scores.	Set unrealistic goals for the current year. (i.e. a student made a 30 last year, don't shoot for a hundred this year.)

Prior year data is a valuable tool for the teacher, the school, and the district.

Teacher

When teaching third grade, depending on the district, there is no prior year standardized testing data to use for goal setting but you can use the data that is available through whatever assessments they are given in second grade along with their student records. For all other grades you can use prior year data to set a goal for them, both individually and as a whole. When students come into third grade, you can often use programs such as Istation and other reading programs to get an idea of the students' ability. Reading and math facts are the biggest concern coming from second grade. Everything else can be worked around.

School

Schools use data to set goals as well. Again, I always set a goal for at least a 10-20% increase from prior year. As I stated before, this is just a goal. Principals may also use data to reassign teachers to other grade levels if they cannot make any significant growth in their current assignment.

District

The district uses prior year data to rate the school as a whole. They also at times may reassign principals and/or administration for inconsistent or lack of academic growth.

State

The state rates school based on academic growth and performance. They use this to decide on funding and the closures of schools.

Goal Setting

Purpose: Goal setting is designed to give you and the student something to work towards. When setting goals be sure to keep it realistic for both yourself and the student. When talking to the students, I would talk percent and not only question numbers. For instance, the goal should be in this format...

> **"Last year you missed_____questions and made a score of _____%. This year we are setting a goal to miss no more than_____questions giving you a score of _____%."**

This enables the student to buy into the process and have an invested interest in it. It is also a goal that is attainable and can be worked toward with every practice standardized assessment.

I usually try to set goals for a 10-20% increase. I use that as a standard across the board. Even if no one else buys into that growth goal, the meeting of my goal affects everyone.

For Goal setting I have a tracking sheet that I use for my class that keeps track of the student progress all year long. I use this tracker for parent conferences, ARDs and any other time I meet with anyone in reference to a student. It is depicted below;

Keep in mind this tracker is for 3rd grade. On the front of the sheet I track the student's fry word level which is a sight word recall sheet that has words from grade 1-10 and the students test over these words every time that they do a practice exam. Then I do a reading fluency test as well. I always try to include the goal on everything that I give to the parents so that they can get an accurate approximation of where their child is. Math computation fluency is yet another objective that I include with the goals so that the parents can see the progress that the student is or is not making. The key measures for this sheet are that the students and the parents can see how the students are progressing in reference to their standardized testing. The objective is to see their scores increase with every administration. I put the passing score of the state assessment since it is not graded on the regular 100 point scale. This helps the parents to not freak out when they see their child getting below 70 though that is the score that we shoot for no matter what.

NOTE: If you are teaching another grade level and you take additional state exams, feel free to add that to your tracking sheet.

The other major objective that I share is the District exams. I track it in the same way and I share that the objective is the same, to see their score increase as the year progresses. During conferences, I am sure to let the parents know the meaning of the beginning of the year exam, middle of the year exam and end of the year exam. This makes the parents feel empowered and informed and it also does something for the student's confidence as well. So when you all set your goal at the beginning of the year, you and the student can see how they are faring throughout the course of the year.

The last objective that I share with the parents is any concerns that I may have. Notice I have the 4 major categories enclosed; behavior, academics, attitude and other. Under the "other" category is where I usually share about attendance concerns.

Dr. Gilbert's Parent-Teacher Team Conference Student Snapshot Sheet

Notes

Glows_____
_____
_____
_____
_____
_____

Grows_____
_____
_____
_____
_____
_____

Signed in attendance

Parent/Guardian_____ Date_____
Teacher_____ Date_____
Administrator_____ Date_____

On the back of the sheet, I use that for conference notes. I use the "glows" for their strengths and positives that are going on and the "grows" for the opportunities that the student has to grow on. I also include parent concerns as well and of course, I allow the parent to sign it, I sign it and I allow an administrator to sign it if need be, but whether they sign it or not I always give them a copy of it as well as the parent for their records.

Data Tracking

Purpose: Data tracking helps the students to see where they need help and also allows you to see where and what interventions are needed at a glance.

Data tracking can be so much fun when done both corporately and individually. I use the same data tracker for both. I have one large wall-sized data tracker for the class and each student has their own as well where they can put their individual data. My data trackers are only for the standardized testing subjects and they look like this;

Semester 1 Math Assessment Data Tracker

Assessment Grade		3.8a	3.23	3.17	3.2b	3.2d	3.15		
100									
90									
80									
70									
60									
50									
40									
30									
20									
10									
		TEKS for Mastery (standards)							

This tracker is a working document that I make at the beginning of the year, one for each testing subject and for each semester. Each week I test the students over one TEK (state expectation standard) and I track the class average and the students take turns coloring in the chart. The students also have a data tracker on their personal data folder that looks identical to this one and they track their own personal scores on their data tracker. I keep this data tracker up on the wall so that at a glance, when I am creating workstations I can see what TEK I need to create a workstation for to increase their proficiency for that standard. We will talk more about this in the intervention chapter.

For data tracking my students have two manila folders. There is one for math and one for reading. They have a data tracker like the one pictured above stapled on the front of each folder. When they take their weekly assessments, they keep those weekly assessments in there as well. This is where their data scores come from and this is the same data that comes from administration.

NOTE: I also keep a digital copy of their scores as well in an excel spreadsheet. This way I always have it if I want to review it at home or when I need to fill out conference sheets.

Now that we have touched on the two biggies; state expectations and standardized testing, let's see how they play out in the classroom as far as planning and implementation.

CHAPTER THREE

LEAD FORWARD

Purpose: *Lead4ward is a Texas program that is created by the Texas Education Agency. This program analyzes the standardized tests and breaks it down in the following manner.*

- State expectations broken into reporting categories
- Reporting Categories broken into TEKS or standards both readiness and supporting.
    - ○ Readiness are the actual standards that are on the test
    - ○ Supporting categories are the skills needed to master the readiness skill.

This resource also lets you know how many questions will be on the test from each category. Not only that, but it has all of the released tests questions and a plethora of other resources that one can use for test prep.

Tricks of the Trade

For each reporting category you can see which ones have the most questions and know that those standards are the ones that you can scaffold into daily instruction.

Consulting with lead forward at the onset of planning is a must for those who want to plan smarter and not harder. Using Lead4ward first makes your efforts intentional in the success of the learning inside of your classroom.

I usually go in this order;

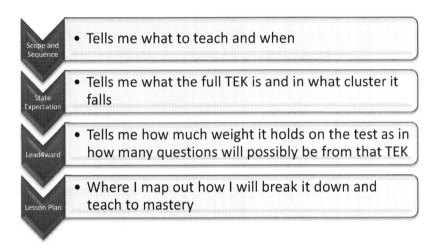

This flow chart is a strategist dream. How much weight an objective holds means a lot when it comes to how long you should teach that TEK and how much emphasis you should place on it in the form of interventions which we will talk about later in the book.

CHAPTER FOUR

SCOPE/ SEQUENCE/ CURRICULUM

Purpose: *The purpose of the scope and sequence is to provide a guide for lesson planning purposes of what to teach when and for how long. The purpose of the curriculum is to tell you what to teach.*

Definitions

Scope- to look at especially for the purpose of evaluation.

Sequence-a continuous or connected series

Cluster-a number of similar things that occur together

Sequence tips:

- Place standards in an order that makes sense. Take the parts and make up a whole. For example,
    - Parts of speech to sentences to paragraphs to essays
    - From operations addition, subtraction, multiplication to division and then move on to word problems and application.

parts of a concept → Whole Unit

Cluster

Sometimes the scope and sequence is provided for you and other times you are responsible for creating it yourself. There are some advantages to both. There are also some tricks of the trade as well.

Scope and Sequence Creation Option Pros and Cons			
Admin Creation		**Teacher Created**	
Pros	*Cons*	*Pros*	*Cons*
More scaffolding at your discretion	Depending on the admin, they may make it harder for you	You have more freedom to teach	It can be time consuming
Creates more cushion for get ahead	Some restrictions may be presented in the implementation	You can put concepts in an order that makes more sense to you	If you have never done it before, it can be intimidating and confusing
Saves time	Sometimes more work is required	You can put your time where it matters most, in the concepts that are more difficult and time consuming.	You still have to keep moving even when the skill is not mastered by the masses.
You are sync'd with other teachers if you are not the only teacher on that grade level	Everyone doesn't teach a concept the same way and different verbiage may be used.	You have more creative control	You have to be more cognizant of the time you spend on a concept.

CHAPTER FIVE

FROM STANDARD TO OBJECTIVE

***Purpose:** To assist the student in visualizing what is to come from the learning experience.*

This is where expectations come from outside the classroom to inside the classroom. The objective is where the learning actually begins. Most schools require for the objective to be posted in a visible place for all to see. The easiest way for a teacher to create an objective is by rewording the standard to an objective that reads;

"TSWBAT_____with _____% accuracy."

Most teachers use this verbiage with the acronym TSWBAT meaning the student will be able to.

A rule of thumb for me is that I put the objective in student friendly terms and we read it together as a class so that the student is aware of not only what we are doing, but also their expected accuracy rate. This is another goal setting method.

CHAPTER SIX

THE SIMPLIFIED ENTIRE LESSON CYCLE

Purpose: Establishes consistency with the learning experience and gives the student standardized expectations for their learning.

The lesson cycle is used to create a sense of normalcy into your classroom and your instructional methods. The more that you draw attention to it and explicitly state what you are doing at a certain point the more the acclimated the kids become to your methodology. I am going to touch on each point of the lesson cycle briefly.

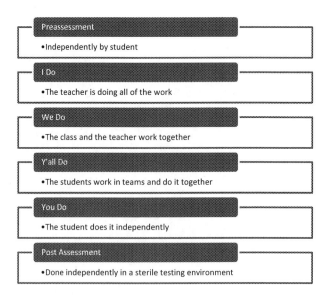

Preassessment
- Independently by student

I Do
- The teacher is doing all of the work

We Do
- The class and the teacher work together

Y'all Do
- The students work in teams and do it together

You Do
- The student does it independently

Post Assessment
- Done independently in a sterile testing environment

Preassessment

Purpose- To see how much background knowledge the student has about the material that you are about to cover. This lets you see if you need to dig deeper and/or supply supporting skills needed to cover the current skill.

Preassessments are what I use as a teaching tool for the "I Do" portion of my lesson cycle. After the preassessment I dive into the language and vocabulary for the unit and take the whole objective and break it into chunks.

I have my own simplified student friendly lesson cycle that I make the students aware of. We do every subject and objective the same way.

- *Monday-Preassessment/I Do*
- *Tuesday-Work Packet "We Do"*
- *Wednesday- Workstations "Ya'll Do"*
- *Thursday-Post Assessment "You Do" / Review*
- *Friday-Weekly Assessment*

I Do

Purpose: All teacher directed. It is where the teacher gives time for vocabulary, algorithms, strategies and most of all introduce applications that will be practiced in the "We Do" phase.

We Do

Purpose: This is where the students and teacher work together to solve the concept. This is what most call "guided practice" with the gradual decline of teacher assistance.

Y'all Do

Purpose: This is another term for the "cooperative learning" piece and "peer coaching." This is also where the students work together and the teacher goes from teacher to facilitator who provides support as needed.

You Do

Purpose: This is all independent work and often times I go over it and use this as a point of review before the final weekly assessment.

Post Assessment

Purpose: Post assessments allow you and the student to see how well the learning was received for the objective.

Post assessments can be given at the end of the day or in preparation for the weekly assessment. I personally give a post assessment quiz on Thursdays because the school administers their assessments on Fridays. This allows me to gauge if there is anything that I need to retouch on before Friday's assessment that is tracked by administration.

I have also worked in districts where they make teachers post assess at the end of every class period. This methodology works as well. They give what they call "Do Nows" at the beginning of class and "Exit Tickets" at the end of class but the methodology is the same.

Weekly Assessments

Purpose: I use weekly assessment data to see how often I may need to scaffold in a particular standard into my instruction rotation or if I need to do a complete reteach. I also use this data to decide my groups for interventions for the following week.

At my current school, administration administers the Friday assessments and they track the data through their own use of scantrons. The school creates the test. We the teachers receive the test on Thursday evenings to administer on Friday mornings. Administration runs the scantrons through the machine and we receive our reports on Monday mornings for our review. From that report I decide how frequently I need to scaffold in that skill into my classroom instruction.

CHAPTER SEVEN

ASSESSMENT TYPES

There are several different types of assessments that I think are worth covering.

Pre-assessment		
Purpose:		
To see how much background knowledge the student has about the material that you are about to cover. This lets you see if you need to dig deeper and/or supply supporting skills needed to cover the current skill.		
Administered by:		
Teacher		
Created by:		
Teacher		
Frequency:		
With each objective		
Form:		
Formal or informal		
Tracked by:		
Teacher and/or student, individually and/or corporately		

Post Assessment

Purpose:
Post assessments allow you and the student to see how well the learning was received for the objective.

Administered by:
Teacher

Created by:
Teacher

Frequency:
At the end of every objective

Form:
Formal or informal

Tracked by:
Teacher/and or student, individually or corporately

Weekly Assessment

Purpose:
I use weekly assessment data to see how often I may need to scaffold in a particular standard into my instruction rotation or if I need to do a complete reteach. I also use this data to decide my groups for interventions for the following week.

Administered by:
School and/or teacher

Created by:
School and/or teacher

Frequency:
Every Week

Form:
Formally

Tracked by:
School, teacher, and/or students, individually and corporately

Benchmarks
Purpose:
Schools use benchmarks to somewhat rate the level of growth that students are experiencing within a given amount of time.
Administered by:
School
Created by:
School
Frequency:
To be determined by school and/or district
Form:
Formal
Tracked by:
School and teacher
NOTE: Oftentimes the district will use released standardized tests to act as their benchmarks.

Standardized Testing
Purpose:
Standardized testing can and should be used for many reason for which we will cover in this chapter. Hopefully after being empowered with the correct way to use the information, you will be for standardized testing as well.
Administered by:
State
Created by:
State affiliated publisher
Frequency:
Annually
Form:
Formal and secured
Tracked by:
State, District and School

The reasons why this is so important is because of the test-driven educational society in which we live, sometimes it is hard for parents to keep up with what test is given by who and what it means. Again I wanted to make this book so simple that even parents can use it and walk away feeling empowered with knowledge on how to help their children as well as ask for what they need and want.

CHAPTER EIGHT

INTERVENTIONS

<u>Purpose:</u> *Interventions are to enable students to get a smaller setting for instruction on a particular TEK or objective.*

Interventions can be done in many ways;

- Inside the classroom by the teacher
- Inside the classroom in workstations
- Outside the classroom by an interventionist or aide

In my other book entitled "Help My Students are Bored and So Am I!" there are a number of interactive activities that I give to use inside the classroom for mainstream instruction or for interventions. You can also use the activities for the mainstream class while you do interventions with the struggling students.

Inside the classroom by the teacher

While the other students are working on other activities and/or assignments, the teacher can be calling a number of students to a table with her to complete intervention efforts and working on a common TEK or objective that they are all struggling with.

Inside the classroom in workstations

If you have a large number of students who are struggling with a concept or those that are border line passing the concept, I would recommend using workstations and placing that objective in a workstation for the students to work on together.

This can be done at any time and does not have to be in the same week that you cover that objective. I do workstations with objectives that I don't want the students to forget or that I know that they struggled with. This knowledge comes from analyzing the data. For reading, I make this a part of my daily questions that I ask after we read any given story. Objective such as inferencing, authors purpose, drawing conclusions and sometimes sequencing are regular struggles of students over the years. Because I know this, I automatically list this as my daily five questions stems when we are in reading. I use the same technique for math using operations and multi-step problems.

Outside the classroom by an interventionist or aide

Again this is district specific, but interventions can be done by the school or by the teacher. I have been on campuses that give the interventionists the curriculum map for them to work from so that the objectives that are being covered in class are also being covered in interventions. I have also seen it where the teacher tells the interventionists what a group of students need assistance on. Another way that I have seen it done is where the campus administration says that there are a set of expectations that campus wide students are struggling with and need assistance on and then the students are chosen by the teacher to go with the interventionists at a prescribed time by administration.

Either method can and will work. Interventions are the greatest methods in the world to help a teacher to fill in gaps. Other forms of interventions to assist in mastery of a skill is;

- Assign as homework
- Create a project or activity for the concept
- Scaffold the concept consistently in everything that you do where it will fit

Note: The more students experience a concept, the more likely they are to remember and master the concept.

CHAPTER NINE

RETESTING

We talked about the 5 general types of assessments in chapter seven, not all of them are able to be retaken.

Type of Assessment	Re-testable
Pre assessment	At the teacher's discretion, though not necessary
Post Assessment	At the teacher's discretion, though not recommended
Weekly Assessment	No
Benchmarks	No
Standardized Testing	Only in retention grades
Retention grades vary by state, but for the state of Texas retention grades are normally grades 5, 8, and 11	

I don't normally recommend retesting because of the measures that I take after analyzing data. What I do is I add those objectives on to future class assessments, or I will implement them into workstations, games, or task cards while keeping an eye on the students who I am aware that are struggling with the concept.

CHAPTER TEN

FORMAL TEST PREP

For me, formal test prep does not begin at the end of the year, it takes place the entire year. This chapter is going to be spoken in laymen's terms because I use this book to assist my parents in knowing how my classroom runs throughout the year as well.

In addition to everything else that you have already read in this book, this chapter will assist the most in trying to understand how my classroom runs.

I liken the school year to pregnancy because often that is what it feels like. The first semester/trimester is a little nauseating and nerve-wracking, but you soon become used to the way things work and you just go with the flow. The second trimester, you feel like you are becoming the expert but you realize that you still need a little help here and there because you understand that you don't know everything. Finally, the third trimester comes and you are ready to deliver. You are not sure what to expect but you know that the task must be done. You are restless and uncomfortable and you just want it to be over with but you realize that time must be of the essence.

Third Trimester	• Spring Break to End of the Year • Thisis formal prep time where there is no more individual concepts, everything looks like the questions on the standardized test.
Second Trimester	• January to Spring Break • The students do more of the work giving back to the teacher what has been taught in the first trimester
First Trimester	• August-December • The students receive a lot of support and the teacher does most of the work of teaching

As you can see by the diagram above, the teacher slowly releases the responsibility and the student's responsibility increases. This is especially a hard pill to swallow for third grade parents because to you, they are still your little babies. Sorry ladies and gentlemen third grade is the age of accountability for the government.

What changes can you expect?

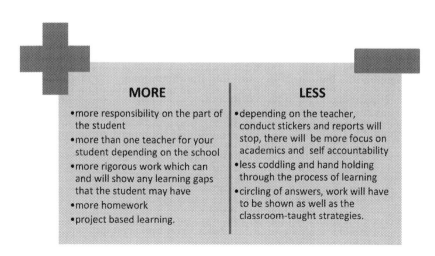

MORE	LESS
• more responsibility on the part of the student • more than one teacher for your student depending on the school • more rigorous work which can and will show any learning gaps that the student may have • more homework • project based learning.	• depending on the teacher, conduct stickers and reports will stop, there will be more focus on academics and self accountability • less coddling and hand holding through the process of learning • circling of answers, work will have to be shown as well as the classroom-taught strategies.

Many parents complain about the workload for students especially because there is a world of difference and a huge jump from second to third grade. With each grade level you can expect more and more responsibility to be placed on the students even from a state level.

This is how they increase responsibility;

Standardized Testing Accountability Increase		
3rd Grade	**4th Grade**	**5th Grade**
• Math • Reading	• Math • Reading • Writing	• Math • Reading • Science
6th Grade	7th Grade	8th Grade
• Math • Reading	• Math • Reading • Writing	• Math • Reading • Science

End of Course Assessments Below May Vary			
9th Grade	**10th Grade**	**11th Grade**	**12th Grade**
English I Algebra I	English II Algebra II Biology	English III U.S. History	

I would have to say that only the best teachers can articulate the method to their madness when it comes to testing. I for one totally understand that I cannot hide it from the students because during testing season the frenzy is on. What I do make a conscious effort to do, especially for third graders since they have never taken the test before, is I equip them on what to expect and every objective ends with the way that they will see it on the test but I don't make that a big issue but very matter of factly. The less of a stress I make of it the less the students will stress about it but they will be aware of how important it is because I mention it.

MY PERSONAL
CLASSROOM METHODOLOGIES

HOW MY CLASSROOM FUNCTIONS

Preparation for Events

Meet the Teacher

As with any other profession, presentation is everything. For my meet the teacher, I prepare a bio much like the one in the back of the book to show myself called and qualified for the tasks and passion of teaching. I create a bio of my qualifications and experience.

I also bring a composition book so that parents can see what I am asking for because I do not use spirals in my classroom for sanity reasons.

I also create a beginning of the year newsletter just for my class. Inside of that newsletter I introduce myself and some of the processes and procedures of my classroom. If I am departmentalized, which means I teach certain subject and my cohort teaches another, I let that be known.

I also try to give a copy of the schedule as well, if the school has that available.

Curriculum Night

For curriculum night in the classroom, I create a PowerPoint that talks about;

- *Communication*
    - ○ The methods in which I communicate; telephone, monthly newsletter, email

- *Homework rotation*
  - ○ Homework is assigned Monday-Thursdays and projects are due every six weeks and as assigned.

- *Break packets*
  - ○ Students receive a work packet to work on over every break which will review various objectives that have already been taught.

- *Projects*
  - ○ Projects are assigned every grading period and rubrics are distributed to go with each.

- *Work Review*
  - ○ Work is given to the students in a "My Work Review Folder" every week on Wednesday for the parents to review.

- *Student Organization*
  - ○ The students will have two folders for my class only. They will have one for their My Work Review Folder and then they will have one for homework.

- *Grades*
  - ○ Grades for my class are put into the system every week by Friday and I always encourage parents to go online and keep tabs of their child's grades.

- *Class Participation*
  - ○ Class Participation is a huge part of my class because we do a lot of interactive activities. Though it is a small percentage of their grade, it can still help or hurt their overall average.

- *Additional Needs that the students may have*
  - ○ In addition to the normal school supply list the students will also need... (this is what I share with parents for curriculum night. I normally always tell the parents to go

ahead and purchase trifold boards for their scholar at the beginning of the year while they are on sale.

- *Materials that we constantly need in the classroom*
  - ○ This is the slide where I always inform the parents of supplies that we use a lot of in our classroom in case they ever want to donate any supplies to the classroom.

- *Materials that the students will constantly need at home*
  - ○ I often encourage the parent to create a consistent, quiet place for the students to do their homework and I also tell them about the supplies that the students will need at home such as a timer, notebook paper, pencil and the like.

Parent Workshops

In the ideal world I would love to have parent workshops where I am able to show parents the strategies that the students learn as well as the algorithms. This has shown to be beneficial, especially in math because parents normally want to revert back to the ways that they know but their method, though it may be accurate, may lack the strategy that the teacher has taught which in turn can confuse the student.

CLASSROOM HAPPENINGS

Behavior

Behavior is never really an issue in my class and I attribute that to my classroom management. I normally handle all behavior issues in my class unless it is a repeated offense or presents a safety issue for myself and all of my students. I do, however, have a behavior guide that I go by.

Level one behavior I handle in my classroom. Level 2 I notify parents and level three, I notify administration.

Levels of Behavior

	Level 1	Level 2	Level 3
Safe, Responsible and Respectful Choices	• Acting angry • Interrupting • Showing frustration inappropriately • Negative actions or words • Not cooperating	• Physical aggression • Disrespect • Disobeying school rules • Inappropriate language • Dishonesty • Other disrespectful, irresponsible, and unsafe choices • Repeated Level 1 behaviors	• Harassment • Stealing • Vandalism • Weapons • Threatening behaviors • Violence • Other disrespectful, irresponsible, and unsafe choices • Repeated Level 2 behaviors

Communication Logs

I try to communicate with my parents in several different ways starting off with a newsletter that they get from my class every month. On top of the newsletter I try to foster a line of communication with my parents. Each time, with few exception, when I contact a parent I keep a log whether it be through email or phone and I log it in. This is for my own records as well as for administration. My log sheet is very simple and is depicted below. I really prefer to communicate via email simply because that is everlasting documentation.

Communication Log

Date	Student Name	Person Contacted	Phone Number	Reason for call	Results

This is a security measure for the parents who say that they didn't know about a matter that we have discussed and as an extra assurance, I also never confer without a witness and I have that witness to initial next to the date.

Parent Tricks of the Trade

Whenever interacting with parents I always try to use the sandwich approach by starting off with something positive then get to the negative and follow up with another positive. I know that as a teacher, sometimes our emotions get in the way, hey, we are all human, but I try to always wait until I am out of my feelings about the matter and then contact parents. Am I always successful? No, however I do try to make it a good practice.

CLASSROOM EXTENSIONS

There should always be extensions to your classroom learning experience. This takes place in many forms such as;

- Projects
- Break Packets
- Repetitive practice project packets
- Homework

Projects

I assign projects every six weeks to my class and the students and parents all love it. This is a time for the parents and students to work together to create something wonderful. I must admit that this is a way that I bring back that old school family time. Do I know that at times the parents take over the project? Yes, but at the end of the day, it still gets them involved. With each project I provide a rubric for the parents and the students. My projects rarely change from year to year which makes it easier for me. All I have to do is change the due dates.

I always try to make sure that I always include the state expectations in state language, but I also provide an objective as well that tells the parents in laymen's terms what the expectation is. Finally, I put the point value for each objective so that the parents can know exactly how I am grading the project. In the appendix, I inserted a copy of one of my rubrics for your review.

Break Packets

For any break that is over three days, including the weekend, I always send home a packet for the students to work on. This is in addition to the added opportunity for the students to work on their projects. The most common break packets are

- Thanksgiving Break
- Christmas Break
- Spring Break
- Summer Break

First Question, Do I grade these page by page? NOOOO!!! However I do provide a completion and /or submission grade for the return of these packets. Remember these packets are not for the teacher, it is for the student. It helps them to stay out of trouble, gives them something to do EDUCATIONAL over the break to keep them somewhat focused on what needs to be done. I especially ensure that I include concepts that the students struggle with as a whole. In every packet I always include math, reading and writing and sprinkled within I put some fun sheets as well that they can just color and have fun with.

Repetitive practice project packets

I also hand out Repetitive practice project packets throughout the year, especially in math for operations and I specifically single out word problems without answer choices. Why do I do this? I am glad you asked! I do this because if forces the students to think and to work the problems and trust the process. I don't really focus on problems with answer choices until I get into test prep because I feel if the student know how the work the problems and can apply the strategy and algorithm then they will learn to be more confident in the work that they do to get the correct answer and the less likely they are to second guess themselves.

I do Repetitive practice project packets for word problems for;

- Addition
- Subtraction
- Multiplication
- Division

- Money
- Time
- Geometry
- Data Analysis

Homework

Homework can be a tricky thing, especially when it comes to time frames of how much times should students spend on homework at home. Here is how I do homework. Statistically for elementary students, grades one to three, homework should take no longer than 15 to 20 minutes per night. For fourth thru sixth the homework should not take more than 15 to 45 minutes. With this in mind, I give home work every night Monday thru Thursday and I leave the weekends for the students to do their projects or to get on computer based learning programs if possible.

Normally I assign one worksheet a night but when I give the students the repetitive practice project packets I give them the packet on Monday and I take it up on Thursday or Friday. The packets are often about 5 pages long which equates to the about the same amount of time.

YEAR END CLOSEOUT DATA FOR PARENTS

At the end of the year, my students walk away with an end of the year closeout data packet that lets their parents know how they grew over the year. This also supports the decision of retention and /or promotion. Again, remember numbers don't lie. When I send home the end of the year data packet it includes a number of things like;

- The completed data sheet that the students have been tracking all year
- Attendance sheets
- Istation printouts
- Recommendation for summer enrichments

Again, this serves as a testament of where the students are currently performing as well as what the expectation will be next year and how to help their child prepare for the higher level of expectations. Yes, I understand that this is above and beyond but in the end most parents appreciate it.

SPECIAL EDUCATION CRASH COURSE 101

My History

Many people ask me, "How did I get my son who has special needs to function so normally in a mainstreamed society?" Well before I get into that, let me give those of you who don't know a little history about that.

I have a son who is at this moment 22 years old. He was born one of a twin and his twin died in my womb. Because of the risk, the doctors did not want to remove the perished twin for fear of hurting the live one. I was placed on bedrest for the remainder of my pregnancy. My son was born at 32 weeks and he only weighed 2 pounds and 14 ounces. There was no knowledge of any issues until after he was born when they told me that he had a piece of his brain missing. The condition is called Agenesis of the Corpus Collosum.

This is where the center piece that connects the two hemispheres of the brain together is actually missing. The report was he will never walk, talk, sit up on his own and a plethora of other nevers. Might I add I was only 18 when this occurred and my mother had just passed away and I had a two year old daughter to add to this madness that was my life. I began seeking all of the support that I could find. I was newly married as well, and neither of us had any idea of what we were doing, but we knew we didn't sign up for this.

One of the agencies that I was working with made arrangements for me to go and see another child with the same diagnoses. He was fifteen years old though. I remember like it was yesterday when I walked into the door and I saw this large child. He was sitting on the coach in a device that looked like a car tire. He needed this device because he could not sit up on his own. He was blind, he had hearing aids, he was in diapers, and naturally he couldn't walk or talk. I looked at his parents, his mother was a stay at home mom just like me. She looked exhausted and rightfully so. I did all that I could to hold the tears in as we began to talk about her day to day life as well as her 15 year struggle to raise this child.

When the conversation was over, I couldn't get out of that house fast enough. I ran to my car and raced to the nearest empty lot which happened to be a grocery store. Now I always had faith, but that day was the day that it got real to me. I sat in my car and screamed to the top of my longs and I told God, "Listen sir, I don't know how I am going to do this and I KNOW I cannot do this alone so listen, I will accept the challenge but THAT I cannot deal with, so promise me that you will help me do this in the most excellent way that neither me nor my baby have to go through that. From that day forward I committed myself to education and research.

I found every agency that I could to help me. Immediately, I got him in physical therapy, occupational therapy, and MY THERAPY. What is "my therapy?" Im glad you asked! It was survival therapy for all parties involved. Now might I add my daughter was a talented and gifted child who was the textbook perfect child to raise, she met all of her milestones early. I quickly learned every child is not going to be the same.

To keep things in perspective, I was only 18, I had no mother to help me because she had passed months earlier, I had married my high school sweetheart, we were broke and was merely trying to survive and I knew nothing about education except the fact that it was important. People told me that I was too smart not to go straight to college but my family was my first priority so I put college, on the back burner for a while until I could get control of my life, if there is such a thing.

My son walked late around two years of age, but that worked to my benefit because that meant that he had no choice but to be still and learn what I was trying to teach him as well as all of his therapists. We created our own family sign language. I would tie a belt around him to assist him in his efforts to walk. Whenever my daughter would sit down to learn, he would be sitting right there in the learning process with us and I wasn't concerned with how much he could and could not do, I just felt that he was sure to get something out of the repetitive talks that I would have with my daughter about her alphabet and her numbers and colors and even when she started reading at the age of three, I had her read to him as well. I figured if I put all of this stuff together in a bowl and mix it up, surely I was going to reap the benefits and guess, what it worked!

It took an act of congress for me to trust someone else to teach my precious gift, but I knew that all of the professionals knew best and way more than I did. We were in Georgia when he started going to school at 3 years old. By the time he went to school, he was walking, potty-trained, and knew how to act in an educational environment, but he talked very little. This is when the practice started for the super bowl of our lives.

All of this had taken a toll on my marriage so now I found myself being a single mom of two children. I had no real family in Georgia so I moved to Texas where all of my family is from. When my son entered into the Texas Education System was when I got the word that he was called, "mentally retarded." I was told this news over the phone at work, devastating, to say the least, but I knew now that I was in the fight of my life FOR his life.

I started again on the search for agencies and resources to help me. Now I was a single mom, raising two children, no college education, and no support from their father and next to no support from my family. I began calling my children and I "the three amigos" because we were in this together and we were all we had. When my son entered into the public education system my role changed from "parent" to "advocate." I had to make some decisions quick and come to some resolutions that kept my son in the forefront of everyone's mind.

I was that parent that would do pop ups at the school. I supported the teacher, but I advocated for my son. If he was wrong he got it, if the teacher was wrong, she got it. Just kidding, no I'm not. Nevertheless, I found it was always the way in which you handled things. Of course when my son entered school he entered school in the special education program due to his diagnosis, but I wanted to continue on the spectrum of not treating him differently. I was very close to his teachers, principals and all of the office staff knew me by name.

Why am I telling you all of this? Because you are the advocate for your child and advocacy starts with education. In this brief chapter, I am going to educate you through the madness of special education without getting too technical and I plan to keep it very simple. First let's look at some of the terms that you are going to hear quite a bit and hopefully the earlier parts of the book will assist you with all of this as well.

Vocabulary

Special Education

Special education programs are designed for those students who are mentally, physically, socially and/or emotionally delayed. This aspect of "delay," broadly categorized as a developmental delay, signify an aspect of the child' overall development (physical, cognitive, scholastic skills) which place them behind their peers. Due to these special requirements, students' needs cannot be met within the traditional classroom environment. Special education programs and services adapt content, teaching methodology and delivery instruction to meet the appropriate needs of each child. These services are of no cost to the family and are available to children until they reach 21 years of age.

504

504 plans are for K–12 public school students with disabilities. Section 504 defines "disability" in very broad terms. That's why children who aren't eligible for an IEP may qualify for a 504 plan. Section 504 defines a person with a disability as someone who:

- Has a physical or mental impairment that "substantially" limits one or more major life activity (such as reading or concentrating).
- Has a record of the impairment.
- Is regarded as having impairment, or a significant difficulty that isn't temporary. For example, a broken leg isn't impairment, but a chronic condition, like a food allergy, might be.

This definition covers a wide range of issues, including ADHD and learning disabilities. However, Section 504 doesn't specifically list disabilities by name.

Having a disability doesn't automatically make a student eligible for a 504 plan. First the school has to do an evaluation to decide if a child's disability "substantially" limits his ability to learn and participate in the general education classroom.

This evaluation can be initiated by either the parent or the school. If the school initiates the evaluation, it must notify the parents and get the parents' consent to evaluate a child for a 504 plan. If the school wants to move ahead without the parents' consent, it must request a due process hearing to get permission to work around the parents' refusal.

When doing an evaluation for a 504 plan, the school considers information from several sources, including:

- Documentation of the child's disability (such as a doctor's diagnosis)
- Evaluation results (if the school recently evaluated the child for an IEP)
- Observations by the student's parents and teachers
- Academic record
- Independent evaluations (if available)

Section 504 requires evaluation procedures that prevent students from being misclassified, incorrectly labeled as having a disability or incorrectly place

Resource Room

Resource rooms are a separate setting, either a classroom or a smaller designated room, where a special education program can be delivered to a student with a disability individually or in a small group. It is for the student who qualifies for either a special class or regular class placement but needs some special instruction in an individualized or small group setting for a portion of the day. Individual needs are supported in resource rooms as defined by the student's IEP. Sometimes this form of support is called Resource and Withdrawal (or pulls out). The child getting this type of support will receive some time in the resource room, which refers to the withdrawal portion of the day, and sometime in the regular classroom with modifications and or accommodations, which is the resource support in the regular classroom. This type of support helps ensure that the inclusion model is still in place.

Intervention

An instructional intervention is a specific program or set of steps to help a child improve in an area of need. Kids can have many different types of needs.

Accommodation

An accommodation is a change that helps a student overcome or work around the disability. Allowing a student who has trouble writing to give his answers orally is an example of an accommodation. This student is still expected to know the same material and answer the same questions as fully as the other students, but he doesn't have to write his answers to show that he knows the information.

Modification

Individualized changes made to the content and performance expectations for students

IEP

If your child receives special education services, he must have an Individualized Education Program (IEP). That's the law. An IEP is an important legal document. It spells out your child's learning needs, the services the school will provide and how progress will be measured.

Goals

These should be realistic, achievable and measurable. The IEP lists the academic and functional skills that the IEP team thinks your child can achieve by the end of the year. Annual educational goals should help your child participate in the general education classroom.

Objectives

If your child has multiple or severe disabilities, the law requires that the IEP list short-term goals. These are also called objectives or benchmarks.

RtI

Response to Intervention (RTI) is a multi-tier approach to the early identification and support of students with learning and behavior needs. The RTI process begins with high-quality instruction and universal screening of all children in the general education classroom. Struggling learners are provided with interventions at increasing levels of intensity to accelerate their rate of learning.

Tiers

There is no single way of doing RTI, but it's often set up as a three-tier system of support. Some school districts call this framework a multi-tier system of supports (MTSS) instead of RTI. One way to understand this tiered system is to think of it as a pyramid, with the intensity of support increasing from one level to the next.

Tier 1: The Whole Class

In the general education classroom, the teacher measures everyone's skills. This is known as a universal screening. The screening helps the teacher work with students in small groups based on their skill levels. All students are taught using methods that research has shown to be effective.

The school will let you know if your child is struggling and will update you on his/her RTI progress. In some schools, the majority of students need Tier 1 instructional support because their reading and math skills are not at grade level.

During the intervention, the RTI team monitors students' progress to see who might need additional support. Many students respond successfully to Tier 1 support and achieve grade-level expectations.

Tier 2: Small Group Interventions

If your child isn't making adequate progress in Tier 1, he'll start to receive more targeted help. This is *in addition* to the regular classroom instruction, not a replacement for it. Tier 2 interventions take place a few times a week during electives or enrichment activities such as music or art so your child won't miss any core instruction in the classroom.

During these extra help sessions, he'll be taught in small groups using a different method than in Tier 1 because the first method wasn't successful. The teacher may also ask you to work with your child at home on certain skills.

The school will monitor your child's progress so it's clear whether the Tier 2 intervention is helping.

Tier 3: Intensive Interventions

Typically, only a small percentage of the class—perhaps one or two students— will require Tier 3 support. In many schools, though, that number is much higher. If your child needs Tier 3 support, it will be tailored to his needs. Every day he'll receive one-on-one instruction or work in very small groups. The groups may include some students who are receiving special education services and who need to work on the same skills.

Your child will continue to spend most of the day in the general education classroom. If he doesn't make adequate progress in Tier 3, it's likely that the school will recommend an evaluation for special education services. This can open the door to individualized teaching, assistive technology and other resources provided at no cost to you.

Safeguards

A Notice of **Procedural Safeguards** is a document that explains the rights of children with IEPs and their parents. It is required by the IDEA as way to insure that parents are clearly aware of their rights

ARD

The letters stand for Admission, Review, & Dismissal committee. This is the name of the committee responsible for making the educational decisions for a student. The parents, or adult students, are members of the ARD committee.

Supplemental Aids

IDEA defines supplementary aids and services as aids, services, and other supports that are provided in regular education classes or other education-related settings to enable children with disabilities to be educated with non-disabled children to the maximum extent appropriate in accordance with IDEA. Some examples include:

- Paraprofessionals or personal assistants for individuals with physical disabilities for assistance in and about school or for transportation
- Instructional support provided by paraprofessionals
- Interpreters for students who are deaf or hearing impaired
- Materials and specialized equipment that help the child remain in the regular education classroom
- Intensive short-term specially designed instruction designed to help keep the student with his non-disabled peers
- Peer tutors or adult tutors
- Regularly scheduled consultation
- Regularly scheduled collaboration among staff

FIE

Full Individual Evaluation. This assessment is conducted by trained professionals to determine if a student has a disability and, if so, the nature and extent of the resulting need for special education and related services.

The Process Simplified

Many parents feel as though they can just walk in off the street and demand testing for their child. From the inside out, my recommendation is to get medical testing first. If there is a need for the school to get involved, the doctor will let you know and will provide paperwork for the school to complete. If the medical analysis is clear, then you can proceed to request testing from the school diagnostician. Before testing takes place the special education coordinator should ask the teacher about completing the RtI process and show evidence of it.

When the RtI process is complete, then if those efforts prove not to be successful, then the school diagnostician steps in and does some formal testing, but the parents have to first provide their consent.

Once that testing is done, then an ARD meeting is held to tell the findings of the assessment and either the child is approved or denied for special education and the reasons for the decision are discussed at that time.

If approved then goals and objectives are set for the students, if declined then the child MAY be placed under 504 and other accommodations may be made for them.

Everyone at the meeting gets a copy of the IEP for execution and then next ARD meeting will be held within a year.

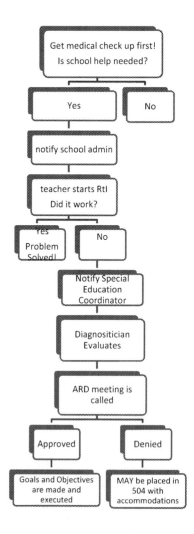

Clearing Up the Misconceptions

There are a few terms that are often misunderstood so let's clear them up;

Accommodation vs. Modification

Accommodations are what are changed in occurrences for the student to be successful. For instance, if a student cannot read well then something can be read to them. With modifications, they are actually changing the instrument such as a test to lessen the stress on a student such as instead of four answer choices, there may be three.

504 vs. Special Education

504 is for students who do not qualify for special education for whatever reason and special education is for students with diagnosed challenges that must be overcome with extensive assistance of some sort.

Goals vs. Objectives

Goals are the numeric value placed on the mastery of the expectations that students should meet. For instance, if a child is to meet a task with 70% accuracy, the percentage is the goal and the task is the objective.

FIE vs. IEP

The FIE is the results to the assessment administered to see if the child qualifies for special education. The IEP is what is created with goals and objectives for the student if they qualify.

CONCLUSION

I hope this book makes the load a little lighter for everyone. As mentioned before, this book serves two purposes. One purpose is to teacher educators how to purposefully drive their instruction in their classroom using data. The second purpose is to educate parents of how my classroom is run and what they can expect from me as well as the methodologies that I use and the reasoning behind it. I am enclosing some screen shots of some things that I use in my classroom that you can use and manipulate to assist you in your efforts as well. An index has been included to make the use of this material much easier for you to use as a resource and reference.

ABOUT THE AUTHOR

Dr. Jennifer Gilbert, ED.D.

Dr. Jennifer Gilbert is a seasoned teacher that has worked throughout the state of Texas and the surrounding areas. She has also worked overseas teaching English as a Second Language. She was born in Lawton, Oklahoma but raised worldwide by a military family but always knew that she wanted to be an educator.

She is an honored high school graduate of Bradwell Institute in Hinesville, Georgia, Class of 1993. She completed the beginning of her college career with a High Honored Associates in Child Development and Business Administration and has completed her Bachelors in the same areas of expertise at Tarleton State University. She also completed her masters in Adult Education and Training at the University of Phoenix. She has her Ph.D. in Christian Education from Northwestern Theological Seminary School and has completed all but her dissertation for her Educational Doctorates (Ed.D).

Dr. Gilbert has taught as the teacher of record for several grade levels from PRE-K through 5th grade in some of the largest districts in the state of Texas to include; Houston, Dallas, and Killeen and even some charter schools and served as substitute throughout her collegiate career for many other grades. Some other professional positions she has or has held is: Youth Pastor, Head of Youth Drama Ministry, Head of Youth Mime Ministry, Head of Christian Education, Pres. Of the YPD (young people's division), Director of Education for Sylvan Learning Center, Special Education Coordinator, part time teacher for Huntington Learning Center as well as the founder and CEO of her own educational consultation company JGM Educational Consultants.

Dr. Gilbert's greatest loves, second to God, are her two children, Damaria and J'Donte (J.J.) Henderson who reside in Texas as the pursuit their own collegiate careers and personal aspirations and her grandson Ethan J'Cean Henderson.

Her famous quote is, "Give me a mind and I will return a miracle." She believes that education is possible for all who desire it. No matter the labels that are placed on an individual. She came to this conclusion when her own biological son was diagnosed with medical obstacles, but she reared him to believe that he can and will learn and despite the labels he graduated from High School on time and he lives a productive, independent life.

She is embarking upon her many works through her Christian books, "Churchin' Ain't Easy" released 2011 and "...And Deliver Us from People..." released in 2012, her book, "For the Perfecting of the Saints: The Five Biblical Ministry Gifts and What They Mean to You" released in 2014 and "365 Revelatory Words for any Given Day: A devotional" She also shares her passion through her educational books entitled, "The Data Driven Classroom Experience" due to release in 2017 along with many others. She has also released gospel cd single "Can I Just Be Me?" full length gospel cd entitled "Love Covers All" with business partner Cacean Ballou. She is also the owner and CEO of

JGM Educational Consultants as well as the founder of Kingdom-Centered Life Changing Educational Conventions that seeks to assist in furthering the education and ensuring the educational success of students of all ages from Pre-K to Post Grads both secularly and in religion. To God be all the glory!

PARENT RESOURCES

Help for _Reading_ Websites

Abcya- http://www.abcya.com/
IStation- http://www.istation.com/
Reading Eggs- https://app.readingeggs.com/login
Starfall- http://www.starfall.com/
Kids A-Z- https://www.kidsa-z.com/main/Login

Help for _Math_ Websites

Think through Math- https://www.thinkthroughmath.com/
IXL- https://www.ixl.com/signin/
Reasoning Minds- https://my.reasoningmind.org/

Help for multiple subjects

Discovery Learning- http://www.discoveryeducation.com/
Study Island- http://www.studyisland.com/
Encyclopedia Britannica- http://school.eb.com/
Brain Pop- https://www.brainpop.com/
Imagine Learning- http://www.imaginelearning.com/
K-5 Learning- http://www.k5learning.com/

In no way is this a complete list of websites but just some of the most commonly used. Simply googling the grade and subject will give you a plethora of resources to use to assist your child.

TEACHER RESOURCES

Pinterest- https://www.pinterest.com/
Teachers Pay Teachers- https://www.teacherspayteachers.com/
K-5 Learning- http://www.k5learning.com/
YouTube- http://youtube.com

Help for _Reading_ Websites

Abcya- http://www.abcya.com/
IStation- http://www.istation.com/
Reading Eggs- https://app.readingeggs.com/login
Starfall- http://www.starfall.com/
Kids A-Z- https://www.kidsa-z.com/main/Login

Help for _Math_ Websites

Think through Math- https://www.thinkthroughmath.com/
IXL- https://www.ixl.com/signin/
Reasoning Minds- https://my.reasoningmind.org/

Help for multiple subjects

Discovery Learning- http://www.discoveryeducation.com/
Study Island- http://www.studyisland.com/
Encyclopedia Britannica- http://school.eb.com/
Brain Pop- https://www.brainpop.com/
Imagine Learning- http://www.imaginelearning.com/
K-5 Learning- http://www.k5learning.com/
*Common Core Sheets- http://www.commoncoresheets.com/

*Even though Texas is not a common core state, nothing says that we cannot use their resources. You just have to look for the objective as Texas is ahead of the common core standards.

There are also a number of websites that you can get from your school and/or district as well.

DOCUMENT TEMPLATES

FINAL END OF THE YEAR CONFERENCE RECAP SHEET (FRONT)

Dr. Gilbert's Parent-Teacher Team Conference Student Snapshot Sheet

Student Name _____ Section _____

End of the Year Data Recap

Final Fry Word Grade Level _____ Final Reading Fluency _____ wpm/130 wpm goal

Days Absent

Excused _____ Unexcused _____

Final Math Computation Fluency

Objective	Goal	Actual Rate
Addition	36/40 in 2 minutes	
Subtraction	36/40 in 2 minutes	
Multiplication	27/30 in 2 minutes	
Division	22/24 in 2 minutes	

STAAR Practice Scores

Subject	September	December	March	April
Math X17 PASS X7 RECOMMENDED X9 ADVANCED				
Reading X3 PASS X5 RECOMMENDED X6 ADVANCED				

Summer Recommendations

Benchmark Data Reading

>70 PASS

BOY	MOY	EOY

Benchmark Data Math

>70 PASS

BOY	MOY	EOY

FINAL END OF THE YEAR CONFERENCE RECAP SHEET (BACK)

Dr. Gilbert's Parent-Teacher Team Conference Student Snapshot Sheet

Notes

Glows

_____

_____

_____

_____

Grows

_____

_____

_____

_____

It has been a pleasure being able to serve you and your family this year!

THROUGHOUT THE YEAR CONFERENCE RECAP SHEET (FRONT)

Dr. Gilbert's Parent-Teacher Team Conference Student Snapshot Sheet

Student Name _____

Date _____ Time _____ Section _____

Data Recap

Fry Word Grade Level _____   Reading Fluency _____ wpm/130 wpm goal

Math Computation Fluency

Objective	Goal	Actual Rate
Addition	36/40 in 2 minutes	
Subtraction	36/40 in 2 minutes	
Multiplication	27/30 in 2 minutes	
Division	22/24 in 2 minutes	

STAAR Practice Scores

Subject	September	December	March	April
Math >87 PASS >76COMMENDED >88 ADVANCED				
Reading >83 PASS >72COMMENDED >83 ADVANCED				

Benchmark Data Reading

>70 PASS

BOY	MOY	EOY

Benchmark Data Math

>70 PASS

BOY	MOY	EOY

Concerns

Behavior   Academics   Attitude   Other

_____
_____
_____
_____
_____
_____
_____

THROUGHOUT THE YEAR CONFERENCE RECAP SHEET (BACK)

Dr. Gilbert's Parent-Teacher Team Conference Student Snapshot Sheet

Notes

Glows _____

_____

Grows _____

_____

_____

_____

Signed in attendance

Parent/Guardian _____ Date _____

Teacher _____ Date _____

Administrator _____ Date _____

RUBRIC TEMPLATE EXAMPLE

My Texas Book Research Project Rubric

Due: December 9, 2016

Assignment Teacher: Dr. Gilbert

Objective	Bloom's Verb	TEKS	Point Value
Student will breakdown a Texas map into the various major regions of Texas.	Analyze	S.S. 3.4A) Geography. The student understands the concept of regions. The student is expected to: (B) identify, locate, and compare the geographic regions of Texas (Mountains and Basins, Great Plains, North Central Plains, Coastal Plains), including their landforms, climate, and vegetation.	/10
Student will compose an organized presentation to include the major symbols of Texas such as the flag, bird, flower, and other important facts about the state of Texas.	Synthesize	S.S.3.17C) Citizenship. The student understands important customs, symbols, and celebrations of Texas. The student is expected to: (A) explain the meaning of various patriotic symbols and landmarks of Texas, including the six flags that flew over Texas, the San Jacinto Monument, the Alamo, and various missions.	/10
Student will describe 3 characteristics of each region of Texas.	Know	S.S. 3.2B) Research Organizing and Presenting Information. The student understands the concept of regions. The...	/10

Objective	Bloom's Verb	TEKS	Point Value
The student will give examples of natural resources in each region of Texas.	Comprehend	B) identify, locate, and compare the geographic regions of Texas (Mountains and Basins, Great Plains, North Central Plains, Coastal Plains), including their landforms, climate, and vegetation. S.S. 3.8) Economics. The student understands patterns of work and economic activities in Texas. The student is expected to: (A) explain how people in different regions of Texas earn their living, past and present, through a subsistence economy and providing goods and services;	/10
The student will construct a timeline of at least 5 important events in Texas history.	Apply	S.S. 3.17) Social studies skills. The student applies critical-thinking skills to organize and use information acquired from a variety of valid sources, including electronic technology. The student is expected to: (C) organize and interpret information in outlines, reports, databases, and visuals, including graphs, charts, timelines, and maps;	/10
The student will choose one landmark	Evaluate	S.S. 4.7B) Social studies	/10

NEWSLETTER TEMPLATE EXAMPLE

BREAK PACKETS COVERSHEET

Thanksgiving Break Holiday Packet

"Dig Into Learning Over the Break"

This packet is due upon your return from the Thanksgiving Holiday. You have 5+ days to complete this activity and it is a project grade so please make sure you turn it in and show strategies.

INDEX

Printed in the United States
By Bookmasters